GW00360810

HISTORY CHART

c. 400–600	Late Roman or sub-Roman mausoleum constructed by holy well
c. 705	Church founded by Aldhelm
909	Church given cathedral status
c. 1180	Present cathedral begun
c. 1230	West front started
1239	Present cathedral dedicated
c. 1255	Chapter House steps and Undercroft started
1306	Chapter House completed
1313–22	Central tower built
1320–40	Eastward extension of quire
1338–48	Scissor arches built
1348	Vicars' Hall completed
1363	Vicars' houses completed (chimneys c. 1470)
c. 1384–94	South-west tower built
c. 1430–36	North-west tower built
1459–60	Chain Bridge and Gate built
1508	South Cloister completed

SAXON
BEGINNINGS

*'The Minster beside the
great spring called Wiela'*

Just behind Wells Cathedral there are five springs, five holy wells, which give the city of Wells its name. These holy wells have drawn people to them for over 2,000 years. Before Christianity came to this land there was probably a shrine here. Later a small Christian chapel was built and the holiness of this site encouraged Ina, King of Wessex, to give land to Aldhelm, the Bishop of Sherborne, who built a church here in AD 705 which was dedicated to St Andrew the Apostle.

Sixty years after the building of that first church, King Cynewulf gave more land to 'the Minster beside the great spring called Wiela [Wells] that the priests there may the more diligently serve only God in the Church of St Andrew the Apostle.' Two hundred years after its foundation, in AD 909, the minster became a cathedral and Athelm was appointed the first Bishop.

We can still trace the alignment of this first cathedral with its head near the holy wells in the east and its doors opening on to the market place in the west. Its last Bishop was Giso (1061 – 88). His successor, John of Tours, appointed by William the Conqueror in 1089, was part of the Norman reorganisation of England. In line with the new thinking he moved the Bishop's throne to Bath, an administrative centre, rather than staying in the holy but remote town of Wells.

These early Saxon beginnings are symbolised by the presence in the present cathedral of the Saxon font which has survived from the first cathedral and is the oldest object in the present building. The font was originally decorated with carvings of saints, standing under rounded arches. Traces of their haloes can still be seen. At some time the figures were chipped off and the arches reshaped so that the font might better match its new setting. The font is still used for Christian baptism, as it has been for over 1,000 years.

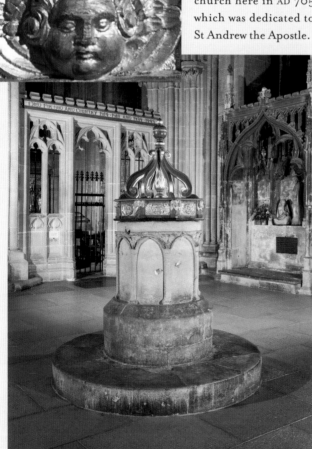

THE SAXON FONT, WITH CHERUB DETAIL FROM THE
JACOBEAN COVER.

THE SPRINGS FEED THE LAKE IN THE GROUNDS OF THE
BISHOP'S PALACE, REFLECTING THE CATHEDRAL.

THE NEW CATHEDRAL

MEDIEVAL FLOOR TILES ARE VISIBLE TODAY.

BELOW: AT THE TIME OF DEDICATION IN 1239, MUCH OF THE WEST FRONT WAS PAINTED IN BRIGHT COLOURS.

Nearly 100 years after Bishop John of Tours moved to Bath, the pendulum began to swing back towards Wells, as the power of this holy place exercised its influence upon men and women of faith. In about 1180 Bishop Reginald ordered work to begin on a new church on a fresh site just to the north of the old cathedral. The new church was planned on a magnificent and ambitious scale. The Bishop and his architect took advantage of the new architectural style which had spread to England and which became known as 'Gothic'. This style used pointed rather than rounded arches and the ceiling vaults were ribbed rather than barrel-like. The church at Wells was the first in England to be planned and completed entirely in this new Gothic style.

Work on the new church began at a point in the present quire on a line between the Bishop's throne and the pulpit and progressed westwards down the nave. In 1208 there was a long break in building which lasted for well over ten years, but eventually the church was completed and, although still not a cathedral, was dedicated in 1239. From start to finish realisation of the grand design had taken about 60 years.

By this time Bishop Reginald had died and in 1206 Jocelyn became Bishop. He was a local man and knew of the holiness of this place, and so sought permission from the Pope for Wells to become once again the seat of the Bishop and for the new church to become his cathedral. But it was not until 1245 that the next Bishop, Roger, was authorised to adopt the title of Bishop of Bath and Wells and to move here, where the Bishop has lived ever since.

So the new Gothic church, splendid with its light and space and its magnificent painted west front, became the cathedral, the seat of the Bishop and a great centre of Christian worship.

RIGHT: THE NAVE FROM THE WEST END, LOOKING EAST TO THE ROOD AND THE GREAT SCISSOR ARCHES AT THE CROSSING.

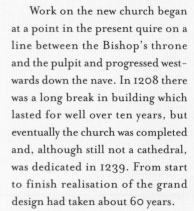

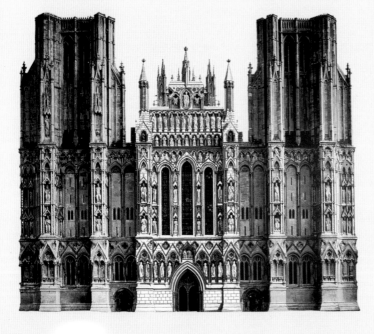

THE QUIRE

The quire is the heart of the cathedral's life. It is where the building began and it is full of light, streaming in from all sides. It has also been full of prayer since its beginnings, for here, almost without a break, the cathedral Chapter has come to pray, day by day, and does so still, today.

After 1320 work was begun to extend the quire eastwards, eventually connecting it to the Lady Chapel which was already in place. By this time the Gothic style had developed further and the horizontal lines of the early quire and the nave had been replaced with vertical lines reaching from floor to ceiling. This different style can clearly be seen in the three eastern bays of the present quire on either side of the high altar. This section of the quire and the beautiful forest of pillars behind the high altar — known as the retroquire, itself one of the glories of Wells Cathedral — was not finished until about 1340.

West of the quire is the great stone 'pulpitum' on which an organ has stood since about 1335. The present instrument was built by Henry Willis in 1857, rebuilt and enlarged in 1909–10, and again in 1973–4. The organ case was completed in 1974.

ABOVE: GILDED WOODEN ANGELS, CARVED IN 1857 BY JAMES FORSYTH, STAND PROUDLY ON THE ORGAN CASE.

ABOVE RIGHT: A LATER MISERICORD, CARVED IN 1664, SHOWING A BOY PULLING A THORN FROM HIS FOOT.

ABOVE: EVENSONG TAKES
PLACE EACH DAY IN
THE QUIRE.

RIGHT: THIS
EMBROIDERY SITUATED
BEHIND THE CANON
PRECENTOR'S STALL
SHOWS KING DAVID
WITH HIS HARP.

The wooden stalls in the quire open their arms to enfold the worshipper in rest and peace. They were made for the canons soon after 1330. Under each hinged seat is what is called a 'misericord', a wooden carving with a small ledge – a discreet prop for clerics standing throughout long services. *Misericordia* is Latin for pity, so these seats 'took pity' upon the clerics and their legs! The stalls with elaborate stone canopies were constructed for the canons in 1848. The rich hues of the modern embroideries in these stalls complement those of the windows above.

THE QUIRE AND THE GOLDEN WINDOW

ABOVE: GREAT CRAFTSMANSHIP AND ATTENTION TO DETAIL ARE EVIDENT THROUGHOUT THE CATHEDRAL AS IN THE ELABORATE HINGE ON THIS DOOR INTO THE QUIRE WHICH WAS MADE IN THE 1300S.

RIGHT: THE QUIRE LOOKING EAST, WITH THE RETROQUIRE AND LADY CHAPEL BEYOND, AND THE GREAT JESSE 'GOLDEN WINDOW' HIGH ABOVE.

High above the quire, breathing its blessing upon the worshipper, is a glorious stained-glass window. It is full of golden yellow glass and so is known as 'the Golden Window'. It was placed here in about 1340, 100 years after the cathedral was dedicated. Its purpose was to demonstrate Christ's fulfilment of the promises of God to the people of Israel. Israel is symbolised by Jesse, the father of King David. It uses the idea of a vine (Jesus said, 'I am the Vine') growing out of Jesse who can be seen lying at the bottom of the window with the vine growing from his side. In the Bible (Isaiah 11:1) it is predicted that the Messiah will come 'from the stem of Jesse'. There are other medieval 'Jesse' windows in England, but this, because of its age and particular colouring, is certainly amongst the finest and most complete.

There is more medieval glass in the windows of the aisles on either side of the quire. Notice in particular the little window depicting the crucifixion high up on the south side where Christ is crucified on a green cross, the tree of life. These quire aisles, which are wide and well lit, were processional ways and are still used for this purpose today. The oldest tombs here are those of the seven Saxon bishops of Wells. These were specially made in the early 1200s when their bones were brought over from the old cathedral. This was part of Bishop Jocelyn's campaign to regain cathedral status for Wells, showing that there had been Saxon bishops here whose memory was revered still in the new church. As we have seen, the campaign was successful and just behind the Bishop's throne, in the south aisle, a list of the bishops shows that the continuity from the earliest times has never been broken.

The Chapter House

The building of this splendid Chapter House resulted from the restoration of Wells to cathedral status. It also marked a new stage in the organisation and independence of the Dean and Canons, known collectively as the Chapter. As the quire was their principal place of worship so the Chapter House, completed in 1306, was built to be their place of business.

The Chapter House in Wells is unique. As you climb the ancient worn steps and turn to the right you enter one of the most glorious rooms in European architecture. It is octagonal in shape and has a central pillar which divides into 32 shafts that soar into the ceiling like a fountain rising from the floor.

The staircase windows contain the oldest stained glass in the cathedral, dating from about 1290. The huge windows of the Chapter House have lost most of their original glass, but a few Resurrection scenes survive high up in the tracery lights. Around the walls are the seats for the members of the Chapter.

Today, the full Chapter only meets here on ceremonial occasions. Day-to-day affairs are in the hands of the executive body known as the Administrative Chapter. From the time of Bishop Robert in the 12th century this comprised five priests – the Dean and four Canons: the Precentor, the Archdeacon of Wells, the Chancellor and the Treasurer. The Dean is Chairman of the Chapter, vigilant in every aspect of cathedral life. The Precentor has charge of the music; the Organist and the choir are directly responsible to him. The Archdeacon of Wells is an important link between cathedral and the work of the Bishop in the diocese.

The Chancellor, originally Chapter secretary, is responsible still for the cathedral's archives and library and promotes theological study. The Treasurer is the guardian of the cathedral's furnishings, vestments and plate, responsible with his team of virgers for ensuring that the cathedral remains a place fit for worship. In recent years these five priests have been supplemented by three lay members, who are known as prebendaries, each of whom is a full and equal member of the Chapter.

This great octagonal room, with its strong central shaft rising from the floor, reminds the Chapter of the biblical command to 'dwell together in unity'.

THIS 1991 CARVING OF A BULL'S HEAD, BY ROBERT ALDRIDGE, IS FOUND ON THE EXTERIOR OF THE CHAPTER HOUSE.

THE SPECTACULAR 32-RIBBED ROOF VAULT OF THE CHAPTER HOUSE IS SUPPORTED BY A CENTRAL PILLAR.

THIS BOSS FROM THE CHAPTER HOUSE CEILING DEPICTS A 'GREEN LADY', SURROUNDED BY FOLIAGE.

THIS GRACEFUL STAIRWAY WORN BY MANY FEET TURNS INTO THE CHAPTER HOUSE.

THE LADY CHAPEL

Mary, the mother of Jesus, has been revered by Christians from the beginning of the life of the Church, but this devotion increased in intensity during the first 200 years of the life of this cathedral. Wells seems to have been particularly fervent in its devotion to Our Lady and for a very long time had two Lady Chapels, one at the east end of the cathedral and one adjoining the cloister.

The Lady Chapel which adjoined the cloister is now lost, but at the furthest and deepest point in the cathedral the present chapel remains, a profound devotional point in the cathedral's life. It was completed in 1326, and was originally separate but precisely aligned with the quire. It is important as evidence of the medieval fascination with sacred geometry – it is an elongated octagon when seen from above, but within it encompasses a circle, the sign of completion.

The upper parts of the Lady Chapel windows and the tracery contain the original glass of c. 1320–6, but much of the rest is a brilliant jumble of fragments salvaged from this and other parts of the cathedral. These windows serve to remind us of the vandalism involved in much English church history and how much medieval beauty was destroyed, notably in the Civil War (1642–7) and during Monmouth's Rebellion (1685). Within the brokenness can be seen signs of hope, especially the beautiful fragment on the north side showing an angel with a trumpet who calls us to live the risen life with Christ.

Today the Lady Chapel is an oasis of peace in a busy cathedral. The furnishings have been simplified and a sense of space created so that the visitor can rest here in prayer and reflection.

RIGHT: VIRGIN AND CHILD STATUE BY A.G. WALKER ON THE EAST WALL OF THE LADY CHAPEL.

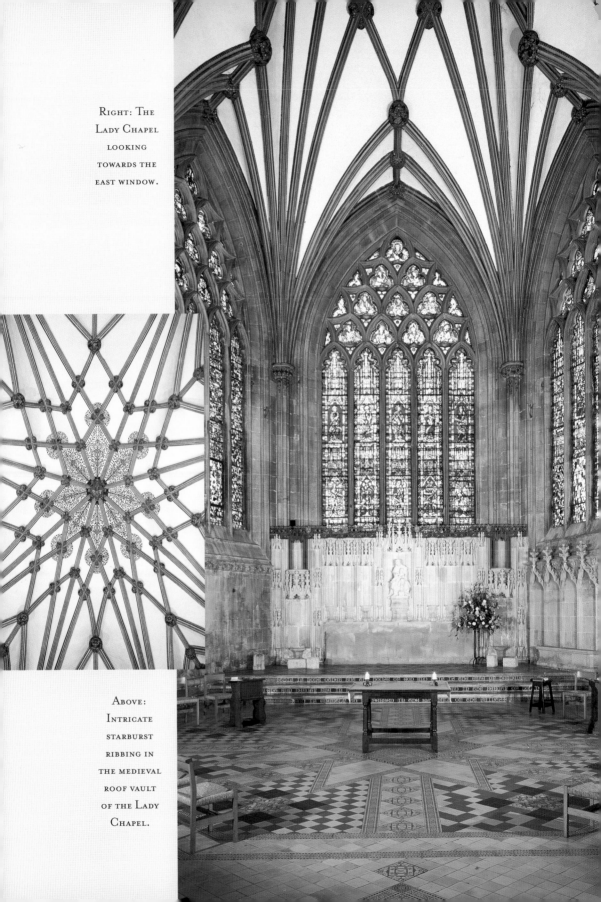

RIGHT: THE
LADY CHAPEL
LOOKING
TOWARDS THE
EAST WINDOW.

ABOVE:
INTRICATE
STARBURST
RIBBING IN
THE MEDIEVAL
ROOF VAULT
OF THE LADY
CHAPEL.

The Nave and the Scissor Arches

LEFT: DETAIL OF THE SUPPORTING SCISSOR ARCHES AT THE EAST END OF THE NAVE.

The nave gives visitors their first impression of the cathedral interior. The two most striking features here are the triforium arches and the great 'scissor' arches at the east end. The triforium is that long row of identical arches just above the pillars on either side of the nave.

The three sets of scissor arches were inserted well over a hundred years after the cathedral was begun, to support the tower when its foundations began to sink. In 1313 Dean John Godelee had added another more elaborate stage to the tower. The result was near disaster. In 1338 the tower began to lean and crack. The spectacular solution of William Joy, master mason, was to construct, during the ten years 1338–48, a scissor arch on each of three sides of the crossing under the tower. Supplemented by hidden buttresses, these arches redistributed the stresses and braced the tower. This dramatic feat of engineering proved a triumphant success. The central tower remains stable to this day. The arches facing the nave are surmounted by the figures of Christ on the Cross with St Mary and St John on either side (known as the 'rood'). These are modern but there were similar figures in the 15th century.

RIGHT: THE SCISSOR ARCHES AT THE CROSSING, LOOKING TOWARDS THE NORTH TRANSEPT.

During the building of the cathedral work on the nave ceased for a time. When work resumed, the overall design continued unaltered, but a sharp eye will detect the 'break'. This can be seen from the change in size of the stone blocks between the columns in the fourth bay from the west end. By the time work resumed bigger blocks could be lifted by more advanced lifting tackle. The decoration of the ceiling, though restored in 1844 and again in 1985, follows the medieval pattern.

The nave was designed as a great space to accommodate processions. Stone benches around the walls for the infirm were the only seating in medieval times. Today the nave is a place of worship, as it never was in the Middle Ages. The principal Sunday service is held here and it is frequently the setting for great services and events drawing hundreds of people.

LEFT: THIS HEAD-STOP IN THE NAVE SHOWS ADAM LOCK, THE MASTER MASON AT THE TIME THE NAVE WAS BUILT. HE DIED IN 1229.

THE WEST
FRONT

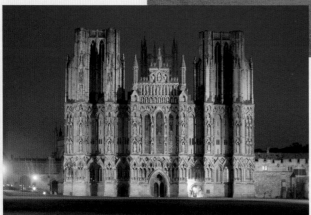

ABOVE & LEFT: THE BEAUTY OF THE WEST
FRONT CAN BE APPRECIATED BOTH BY DAY
AND BY NIGHT.

RIGHT: DETAIL SHOWING THE RISEN
CHRIST STATUE (1985) CARVED BY
DAVID WYNNE.

The external west front of the cathedral is one of the most celebrated of its kind. It is like an elaborate altar screen, containing an array of limestone carvings which spread across the width of the nave and the towers on either side. It is full of carvings of people: bishops, saints, men and women. It contains one of the greatest collections of medieval statuary anywhere in Europe. When the cathedral was dedicated in 1239 much of it was painted in reds, greens and golds, traces of which can still be seen. Even with the colours lost and many figures missing or weather worn, it is still the most glorious array. Mary, the mother of Jesus, is directly above the main door while Christ himself is at the top of the west front. The little niches are full of carvings of incidents from the Bible. At the first level the Old Testament scenes are to the right and New Testament scenes to the left. Above these are saints and bishops while above them are Resurrection scenes; so from the ground upwards there is a movement from time through to eternity.

Recent research shows that this great west front came into its own on important liturgical occasions, particularly Palm Sunday. On that great feast, which cele-brates the entry of Christ into Jerusalem, the procession of worshippers coming across the cathedral green entered the cathedral as the new Jerusalem. They were greeted by the sound of trumpets and the voices of choristers emerging from the specially carved holes which can still be seen between the figures.

At the top of this great front, in the central section, above the angels, are the twelve Apostles with St Andrew, the patron saint of the cathedral, in the middle. He stands slightly forward of the others and is holding his cross (like an X) in front of him. Above him is Christ. Flanked by six-winged seraphim, this figure was put up in 1985 to replace what remained of the medieval original. With one hand raised to bless while the other extends an open palm, the Lord of the Church welcomes the pilgrim.

THE CLOISTERS AND THE LIBRARY

Although Wells was never a monastery it nonetheless has a cloister. This sheltered walkway is a place for quiet reflection and study. It encloses the green lawn of the Palm Churchyard, the burial ground for the cathedral clergy. Here too there is a 'Dipping Place'. This leads down to water which flows through a conduit under the cloister from the wells to the town, laid by Bishop Bekynton in the 15th century.

Above: Studying in the cathedral library.

Right: Looking north along the 15th-century East Cloister.

Above: Now housed at Wells, this psalter was made for Hailes Abbey in Gloucestershire in 1514 by the Flemish scribe and illuminator Peter Meghen (known as Peter the One-Eyed).

The east cloister has always been the Bishop's entrance to his cathedral. Its graceful Early English doorway is one of the few survivals from the original, narrow 13th-century cloisters. Halfway down the East Cloister is the door into the Camery Garden. At the end of the Camery Garden the visitor can peep through a hole in the wall to see the water springing up from one of the wells which give the city its name.

Medieval cathedrals were centres of learning and it is thought that much of the teaching went on in the cloisters. Wells Cathedral has had its own school from very early days. It is not surprising therefore that the cathedral acquired many books, and by the 1400s needed a proper library to house them. Bishop Bubwith, who died in 1424, left 1,000 marks to build a library over the east cloister.

The library is one of the longest of its period in England. Its many small windows are characteristic of medieval schools and libraries. There are about 6,000 books, mainly of the 16th–18th centuries, and the archives of the Chapter from the 10th century to the present day. Some of the books are still chained to the book presses which, with their desks, were fitted in 1686.

The books disclose the interests of the clergy of the time: not only theology, but also law, medicine, travel, languages, botany and mathematics. Bishop Hooper (1703–27) donated a large collection of books devoted to the understanding of Judaism and Islam, an early indication of how important dialogue with other faiths would become.

Today the library is being developed to allow more people to come and study here, thus enabling the cathedral to become once again a centre of Christian learning.

THE CLOCK

By the end of the 14th century the liturgical life of the cathedral was busy and there were more services than ever. Precise timekeeping became essential. Therefore, like so many other cathedrals, Wells installed a clock. The uniqueness of the clock at Wells is that its face is still here, 600 years after its installation. It is first mentioned in 1392. Its original mechanism is now in the Science Museum in London, replaced by an 1880 movement behind the 14th-century painted clock face.

It is a full 24-hour clock, starting with 12 noon at the top and moving through midnight at the bottom back to 12 noon again. The inner circle tells minutes in a similar fashion. The third, inner dial indicates the number of days which have elapsed since the last new moon. Meanwhile, the knights above the clock rotate every quarter hour. Jack Blandiver, the mysterious figure high up to the right, rings the bells. On the central face a painted disc changes to show the waxing and waning of the moon.

LEFT: THE CLOCK IN THE NORTH TRANSEPT, AND DETAIL OF THE 600-YEAR-OLD FACE.

The clock still fulfils the same function today as it did when it was installed, services beginning 'when the clock strikes'.

The statue of the risen Christ beneath the clock was carved in yew wood by Estcourt Clack in 1954 and reminds those watching the clock that Christ is the Lord of all time.

ABOVE: ONE OF THE FOUR JOUSTING KNIGHTS WHO REVOLVE AT EVERY QUARTER-HOUR.

LEFT: JACK BLANDIVER STRIKES BELLS AT EVERY HOUR AND QUARTER.

THE CAPITALS

BELOW: A CAPITAL FROM THE NAVE OF A DEVIL HEAD WITH ASS'S EARS. THIS THEME IS ECHOED IN ONE OF THE MISERICORDS OF THE QUIRE.

BELOW RIGHT: AN EXAMPLE OF 'STIFF LEAF FOLIAGE' CARVING IN THE CAPITALS OF THE QUIRE.

The carvings in the cathedral at the tops of the pillars (the 'capitals') are very famous. They are among the best of their kind, showing scenes from medieval life. You can find someone removing a thorn from his foot, a man with toothache, and a cobbler mending shoes. On the column nearest to the end of the south transept the carvings at the top tell the story, as you move around in an anticlockwise direction, of some grape stealers and their capture and punishment. This is like a strip cartoon in stone.

A careful look will reveal a development in the carvings, a process of discovery by the masons of their skill, which is reflected in the growing variety and complexity of the designs. The capitals in the quire show very little inventiveness, being mostly simple 'stiff leaf' designs. But by the time the nave was built there is much more — a fox stealing a goose, a spoonbill eating a frog, a man with extremely large ears, and many others. There are faces, animals, birds and even some which cannot be deciphered. There is a lizard, what looks like a monkey, indeed a veritable explosion of life. The cathedral stonemasons obviously believed that the church building should reflect their own good humour and delight in the creation.

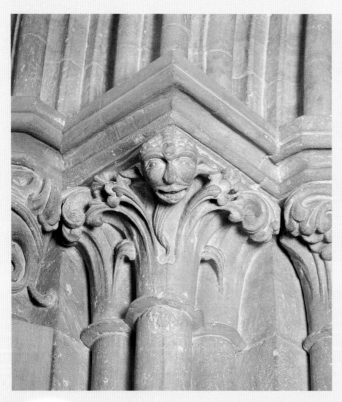

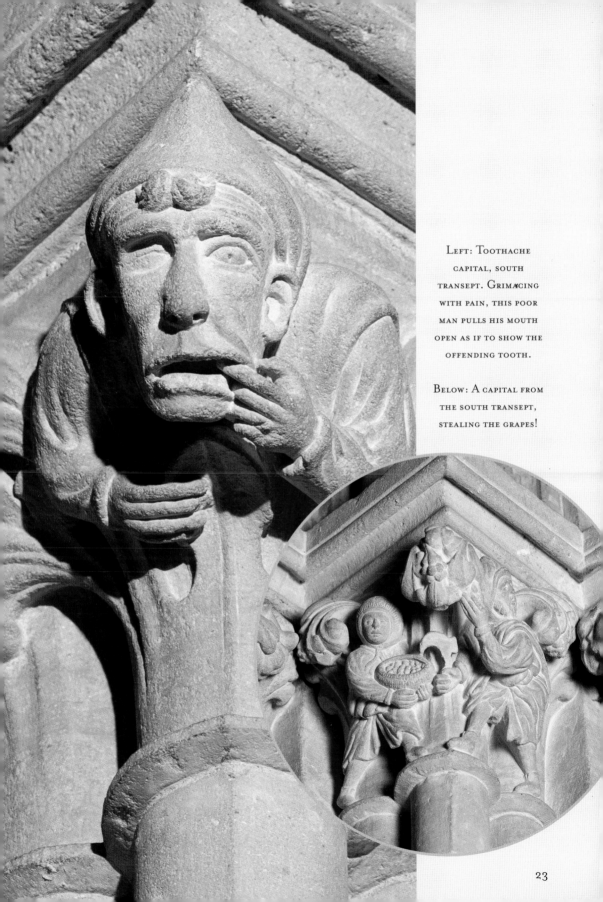

LEFT: TOOTHACHE
CAPITAL, SOUTH
TRANSEPT. GRIMACING
WITH PAIN, THIS POOR
MAN PULLS HIS MOUTH
OPEN AS IF TO SHOW THE
OFFENDING TOOTH.

BELOW: A CAPITAL FROM
THE SOUTH TRANSEPT,
STEALING THE GRAPES!

BISHOP THOMAS KEN

The nearest that Wells Cathedral has to a saint is Thomas Ken, who was Bishop here from 1685 to 1691. He lived in troubled times and was a very saintly man. He is not buried in the cathedral, but in Frome, 16 miles (24km) away. There is a stained-glass window depicting him in the north quire aisle and the cathedral library holds his own handwritten prayer book as well as a large part of his library.

Above all Ken was a man of prayer. When he was a Fellow of Winchester College he wrote a special book of prayers for the pupils there called *A Manual for Winchester Scholars*. His own handwritten *Book of Hours* shows how he learned from the traditions of the Church and how carefully and lovingly he said his prayers. He also wrote hymns, many of them still in use today.

Ken was also a man of principle. He refused to allow Nell Gwynne, Charles II's mistress, to stay in his house during the King's visit to Winchester. Later, an even greater principle was at stake when he refused to accept the Declaration of Indulgence and with seven other Bishops was imprisoned for a short time in the Tower of London. When James II fled England and William was crowned King, Ken refused to swear the oath of loyalty to William as he believed James was still the lawful King, even though he had been deeply unhappy at much that James had done. For this Ken was deprived of his bishopric and ended his days at Longleat.

Bishop Ken showed his deep pastoral concern when in 1685 many of those who had supported the Duke of Monmouth in his rebellion against James II were condemned to death or deportation by the hard-hearted Judge Jeffreys and were imprisoned in the cloister of the cathedral. The bishop visited these condemned men regularly and appealed to the King for clemency towards them.

THE THOMAS KEN EMBROIDERY IN THE QUIRE, *PASTOR DILECTISSIMUS PIETATE CRAVISSIMUS*: A BELOVED SHEPHERD; A SAINTLY CHARACTER.

God, our heavenly Father, make, we pray, the door of this Cathedral Church wide enough to welcome all who need human love and fellowship and a Father's care; but narrow enough to shut out all envy, pride and lack of love.

Here may the tempted find help, the sorrowing receive comfort, the careless be awakened to repentance, and the penitent be assured of your mercy; and here may all your children renew their strength and go on their way in hope and joy; through Jesus Christ, our Lord.

Amen.

AN
ENGRAVING OF
THOMAS KEN.

THE THOMAS KEN WINDOW WAS
ENTIRELY PAINTED IN ENAMELS BY
P. AND N. WESTLAKE. IT WAS ERECTED
IN 1885 TO CELEBRATE THE BICENTE-
NARY OF KEN'S CONSECRATION AS
BISHOP OF BATH AND WELLS.

BISHOP KEN'S HAND-
WRITTEN PRAYER BOOK.

Awake, my soul, and with the sun
Thy daily stage of duty run;
Shake off dull sloth, and joyful rise
To pay thy morning sacrifice.

The Vicars Choral and Vicars' Close

Above: Inside the Vicars' Hall.

Above right: Vicars' Close and the Close Chapel beyond.

Right: The Chain Gate links Vicars' Close to the cathedral.

In Wells the men who sing in the cathedral choir are known as 'Vicars Choral'. They have been an integral part of cathedral life since the 12th century. Who they are and what they do will be understood by realising that vicar means deputy. Canons, not bound to the cathedral as monks to a monastery, appointed deputies (vicars) to undertake duties that they themselves could not or would not perform. Then, as now, music was central to cathedral worship and vicars were chosen for their skill in singing — hence 'Vicars Choral'.

In the 14th century Bishop Ralph of Shrewsbury found that the vicars were living in poor circumstances, so in 1348 he formed them into a college, and drew up rules of practice. He built Vicars' Close to house them, and Vicars' Hall where they ate together and transacted business.

Vicars' Close originally consisted of 42 small houses in two rows with a chapel for the vicars at the far end.

It was something like an Oxford or Cambridge college. Religious upheavals in the 16th century reduced the number of Vicars Choral, but they were now free to marry. Houses were put together into larger dwellings to accommodate their families. The cobbles and walled gardens came later giving the appearance of a medieval street.

Through all of these changes, the work of the Vicars Choral continued as it does today. The men of the choir still live in Vicars' Close, as do other members of the cathedral foundation. Along with the choristers the Vicars Choral sing every day in term time, and with their families form an important part of the cathedral community.

The Organist is also Master of the Choristers and, under the Precentor's direction, responsible for the cathedral's musical life. Appropriately, he too now lives in Vicars' Close. Some of the houses in Vicars' Close are used by the Cathedral School, which has a continuous history since the foundation of the medieval choir school. It now provides for boys and girls of all ages, and is famous as a specialist music school. It occupies many of the historic houses in The Liberty once occupied by the canons.

This very fine corbel of a salamander (some say a lizard) eating currants is found in the east aisle of the north transept.

THE CATHEDRAL TODAY

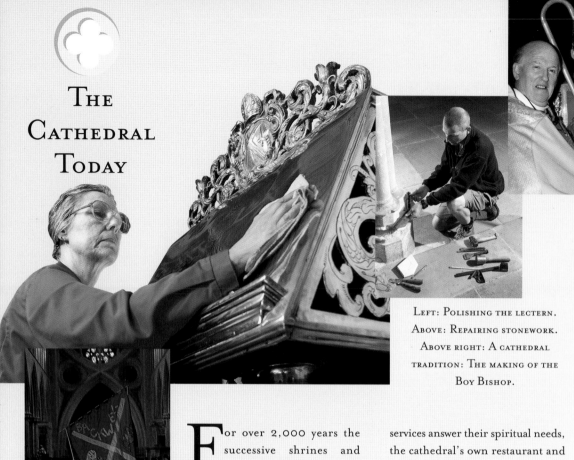

Left: Polishing the lectern.
Above: Repairing stonework.
Above right: A cathedral tradition: The making of the Boy Bishop.

Primary school children at the end of term service.

Changing the altar frontal.

For over 2,000 years the successive shrines and churches on this holy site 'next to the great spring' have been a sign of God's nearness and have drawn people into God's presence. Today this great cathedral fulfils the same purpose. It is a place of divine attraction, calling the visitor to see the love of God, as shown by Jesus Christ, hidden in all things.

So the cathedral remains above all a place of prayer. At least twice a day, every day of the year, the Chapter and the cathedral community, together with worshippers from far and near, come together to give thanks to God and to pray for the needs of the world.

Each year well over 400,000 visitors are welcomed by a small army of volunteers and cathedral employees. Whilst the three daily services answer their spiritual needs, the cathedral's own restaurant and shop meet their physical needs. St Benedict said that the needs of the visitor to the monastery must come before everything else, and here in Wells the same principle is followed.

But it is not just the visitor who comes to the cathedral. The faithful of the Diocese of Bath and Wells come to hear their Bishop preach. Here new priests are ordained to carry the message of God's love to the people of Somerset.

But all the time, in the midst of all the business of a great house of God, a quiet chapel can be found, and people sitting, praying or lighting candles. The cathedral is a busy place, but it strives to preserve an atmosphere of peace and serenity, drawing us to wait upon God and to renew our strength in him.

LEFT: ARRANGING
THE FLOWERS.
BELOW: A TIME FOR
PRAYER.

ACKNOWLEDGEMENTS

The text was written by Canon Melvyn Matthews,
Chancellor of Wells.
Edited by John McIlwain.
Designed by Simon Borrough.

All photographs © Jarrold Publishing (by Peter Smith of
Newbery Smith Photography and Mark Slade) except for:
Chorley & Handford: inside front cover – p.1; Wells
Cathedral (by Richard Neale): p.6 top, p.10 top, p.25
top; Wells Journal: p.28 top, centre left.

The artist's impression of the medieval west front on p.4
is the work of Jerry Sampson.

Text © Wells Cathedral.

Publication in this form © Jarrold Publishing 2002.

No part of this publication may be reproduced by any
means without the permission of Jarrold Publishing and the
copyright holders.

Pitkin Guides is an imprint of Jarrold Publishing,
Norwich.

Printed in Great Britain.

ISBN 1 84165 093 5   1/02

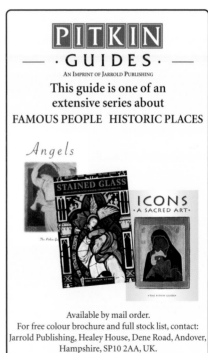

PITKIN
· GUIDES ·
AN IMPRINT OF JARROLD PUBLISHING

**This guide is one of an
extensive series about
FAMOUS PEOPLE   HISTORIC PLACES**

Angels

STAINED GLASS

ICONS
· A SACRED ART ·

Available by mail order.
For free colour brochure and full stock list, contact:
Jarrold Publishing, Healey House, Dene Road, Andover,
Hampshire, SP10 2AA, UK.
Sales: 01264 409206
Enquiries: 01264 409200 Fax: 01264 334110
e-mail: heritagesales@jarrold.com
website: www.britguides.com

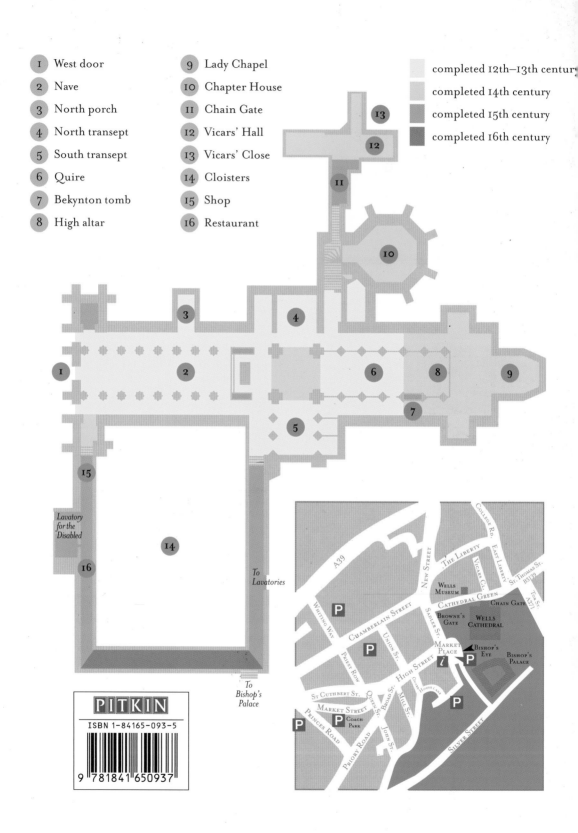

1 West door
2 Nave
3 North porch
4 North transept
5 South transept
6 Quire
7 Bekynton tomb
8 High altar

9 Lady Chapel
10 Chapter House
11 Chain Gate
12 Vicars' Hall
13 Vicars' Close
14 Cloisters
15 Shop
16 Restaurant

completed 12th–13th century
completed 14th century
completed 15th century
completed 16th century

Lavatory
for the
Disabled

To
Lavatories

To
Bishop's
Palace

Map street labels:

A39
WHITING WAY
NEW STREET
COLLEGE RD.
THE LIBERTY
EAST LIBERTY
VICARS CL.
ST. THOMAS ST.
B3139
Tor St.
A371
WELLS MUSEUM
CATHEDRAL GREEN
CHAIN GATE
CHAMBERLAIN STREET
SADLER ST.
BROWNE'S GATE
WELLS CATHEDRAL
UNION ST.
PRIEST ROW
MARKET PLACE
BISHOP'S EYE
BISHOP'S PALACE
ST. CUTHBERT ST.
HIGH STREET
CHAMBER HOUSE LANE
MARKET STREET
QUEEN ST.
BROAD ST.
MILL ST.
COACH PARK
PRINCES ROAD
PRIORY ROAD
JOHN ST.
SILVER STREET

PITKIN
ISBN 1-84165-093-5
9 781841 650937

EDINBUR

CW00327718

A Brief History

prehistory
Stone Age and
Bronze Age
hunters
occupy the
crag.

1018
Malcolm II reclaims
Edinburgh and pushes
the Scottish boundary
further south.
1128
David I founds
Holyrood Abbey.

15th century
Nor' Loch is created and a
city wall built. Edinburgh
becomes capital of
Scotland.
1501
James IV modifies the
guesthouse of Holyrood
Abbey to create a palace.

1513
James IV and
army are anni
at Flodden Fie
1544
Edinburgh is
ravaged on th
orders of
Henry VIII.

638
Din Eidyn falls to
the Angles of
Northumbria and is
thereafter called
Edinburgh.

1295
Scotland's 'Auld
Alliance' with
France begins.
1296
Edinburgh Castle is
sacked by Edward I
of England.

1314
Robert the Bruce orders
that the castle is
recaptured and
dismantled.
1322
The English sack
Holyrood Abbey.

Since the beginning of history, Din Eidyn, the fort on the hill-slope, has been fought over by those who have desired control of the region. The Celts, Angles, Britons and Vikings all tried to stake their claim, as did the Scots from Western Ireland after whom the country is named. In a history as turbulent as the Scottish weather, the castle was besieged, reduced to a ruin and rebuilt with horrible regularity in the persistent conflict between the Scots and the English.

Yet from this troubled town beset by national strife and religious rebellion has flourished one of the most distinguished and classically beautiful cities in the world. For since 1746 Edinburgh has known peace and security, an atmosphere that has nurtured the development of ingenious thinkers and prodigious writers, and enabled the town to break out of its defences and expand in exceptional style. Visitors to Edinburgh today find an exciting city, built on hills and linked by outstanding bridges, that baffles with its changing levels, astonishes with its unexpected views and sobers with the dourness and indomitability of its mighty castle.

1559
The Protestant John Knox becomes minister of St Giles'.
1582
Edinburgh University is founded.

1566
Rizzio, secretary to Mary Queen of Scots, is murdered at Holyroodhouse.

1603
James VI's accession to the English throne. Royal Court moves to London.
1638
The National Covenant is signed, renouncing popery.

1750–1800
Edinburgh is known as a brilliant intellectual and artistic centre.
1759 onwards
Nor' Loch is drained.
1767
The first New Town is started.

1947
Edinburgh Festival is founded.
1998
The Museum of Scotland opens.
1999
Elections are held for the new Scottish Parliament.

1561
Mary Queen of Scots returns from France a widow. Scotland is declared a Protestant country.

1661–88
About 100 Covenanters are hanged.
1707
Scottish Parliament is dissolved.
1745
Jacobites attack Edinburgh.

1771
Walter Scott is born in Edinburgh.
1850
Robert Louis Stevenson is born in Edinburgh.
1858–72
Greyfriars' Bobby keeps a vigil by his master's grave.

Edinburgh Castle

No one is quite sure when the first fortress was built on the volcanic rock of Edinburgh, but it seems unlikely that such a superb site would have been ignored by prehistoric settlers. The first records of Din Eidyn appear shortly before AD 600, when warriors of the Lothians were annihilated by the Angles of Northumbria. Edinburgh Castle was frequently the site of terrible war and bloodshed from that time until the last attack, in 1745, when Bonnie Prince Charlie attempted to regain the throne. Today this historic monument is Scotland's greatest tourist attraction, offering fascinating insights and superb views of the city and beyond.

GATEHOUSE

Flanking the gatehouse entrance to the castle are the statues of William Wallace, great Scottish leader of the late 13th century, and King Robert the Bruce. Bruce was responsible for recapturing the castle from the English in 1314 by ordering 30 men to ascend the precipitous north face of Castle Rock to take the fortress by surprise. He immediately dismantled the castle in order that it could not be occupied again. Above the arch the phrase *Nemo Me Impune Lacessit*, meaning 'no one offends me with impunity', warns off potential aggressors.

ONE O'CLOCK GUN

The one o'clock gun, originally a time signal for shipping on the Forth, has been fired from the northern defences of the castle every day except Sundays for around 150 years.

Edinburgh Castle

THE PALACE

Visitors to this greatly altered 16th-century royal residence may view the tiny panelled bed chamber where Mary Queen of Scots gave birth to the future James VI of Scotland (James I of England), and the Crown Room containing the ancient Honours of Scotland.

ST MARGARET'S CHAPEL

Built in the 12th century by David I in honour of his mother, Queen Margaret, this tiny Romanesque chapel in the Upper Ward is the oldest building in Edinburgh. Margaret, wife of Malcolm III, died in the castle in 1093 after receiving news of her husband's death in battle.

SCOTTISH NATIONAL WAR MEMORIAL

Beautifully adapted 18th-century barracks commemorate those Scots who lost their lives in the two World Wars.

St Margaret's Chapel window

MONS MEG

In 1457 James II received a gift of Mons Meg, a giant muzzle-loaded siege gun capable of firing its huge stone cannonballs to a distance of 1½ miles. However, its great weight meant that, even with enormous manpower, it could only be moved a distance of 3 miles a day, and by the middle of the 16th century it was consigned to the castle ramparts and restricted to firing salutes. When Mons Meg was last fired in 1681 its barrel burst and it was dumped. It is now displayed in the vaults.

GREAT HALL

Built as a banqueting and assembly room in the early 16th century, the Great Hall has since been used as barracks and a hospital. It was restored in a rather imaginative medieval style in the Victorian era, but the splendid hammer-beam roof and fine decorated stone corbels are original.

The Royal Mile – Castle Hill

Descending the rocky ridge from the castle to Holyrood Palace is the Royal Mile, a mile-long chain of streets which forms the backbone of the Old Town, met along its length by many fascinating closes. Through the centuries this extraordinarily historic street has seen a mingling of people from all walks of life: beggars and murderers, fishwives and foreign traders, royalty and men of genius.

The Royal

THE WITCHERY

WITCHES WELL

A decorated fountain on the west wall of the Tartan Weaving Mill commemorates the women who were convicted of witchcraft and burned at the stake here in front of the castle. To determine whether or not an elderly or eccentric woman was a witch, she would be tied up and thrown into the Nor' Loch to the north of Castle Rock: if she floated she was guilty and therefore burned, and if she sank and drowned she was innocent.

RAMSAY GARDEN

Perched at the top of Princes Street Gardens (▷ 25), this distinctive white and red building of residential flats was built in 1892–94 by Sir Patrick Geddes, an early and much-admired town planner who believed in fostering neighbourhood and community spirit.

CASTLE ROCK

Castle Rock and the Royal Mile are a superb example of the geological feature known as a 'crag-and-tail'. The violent eruption that occurred so long ago formed a huge conical volcano which eventually became extinct. During the Ice Age, the flow of glaciers from the west to the east was interrupted by the huge eminence. The ice eroded the soft sedimentary rocks from the volcano's surface and created the valleys to the north and south that are now Princes Street Gardens and the Grassmarket. The basalt 'crag' that remained protected the softer rock to its east, and the separated streams of ice did not merge again until near Holyrood Palace, forming the 'tail' that is the Royal Mile.

TARTAN WEAVING MILL

A renovated reservoir is home to the Edinburgh Old Town Weaving Company, where visitors may learn the history of highland dress and watch tartan being woven on clattering machinery.

CAMERA OBSCURA

Situated at the top of the Outlook Tower, the 1853 Camera Obscura transfers live moving images of the city onto a concave viewing table. On the floors below it are fascinating displays of historic Edinburgh photographs, pin-hole cameras and holograms.

SCOTCH WHISKY HERITAGE CENTRE

Visitors to the centre learn, by means of a film and a friendly ghost, how whisky is made, and after a barrel-car ride through whisky's social and industrial history are offered a free 'dram' at the bar. The gift shop sells an amazing selection of whiskies, some of them very rare.

TOLBOOTH KIRK

This Victorian Gothic church, which once served the Gaelic community of Edinburgh, now houses 'The Hub', the administrative centre for the Edinburgh Festival (▷ 16–17). The building's octagonal spire is the highest in Edinburgh.

Ramsay Garden

The Royal Mile – Lawnmarket

This was a medieval market place, where the daily dairy and meat stalls gave way to linen and woollen cloth once a week. Many Scottish aristocrats and rich merchants chose to live in this area, which was also home for a while to two great literary men, James Boswell and Robert Burns.

Lawnmarket

CLOSES, WYNDS AND COURTS

Early houses that fronted onto the Royal Mile were extended into the courtyards behind, with access provided through archways or narrow passages. Prevented from expanding further outwards by the steep slopes, the tenements, or 'lands', were forced to develop upwards, sometimes to as high as ten storeys. The broad and colourful social mix of people that lived here were exposed to filthy conditions, which resulted in frequent fevers and plagues. With a warning cry of "Gardy loo!" (from the French *gardez l'eau*), slops and waste of all kinds were thrown from the windows to stink and rot in the closes below, along with the dung of the pigs that were kept there. Now rehabilitated and rebuilt, the closes follow their medieval patterns and retain their distinctive character.

Gladstone's Land

GLADSTONE'S LAND

Gladstone's Land, the early 17th-century shop and house of the merchant Thomas Gledstanes, has been skilfully restored and furnished in the style of the period by The National Trust for Scotland. Its interesting rooms are open to the public.

Writers' Museum

WRITERS' MUSEUM

The restored grand mansion of Lady Stair's House, built in 1622, is home to the fascinating Writers' Museum, which celebrates the lives and works of Scotland's three greatest literary figures, Burns (▷ 20), Scott (▷ 24) and R.L. Stevenson (▷ 26). Makar's Court, outside the house, features inscriptions commemorating famous Scottish writers.

DEACON BRODIE'S TAVERN

This attractive pub is named after Deacon William Brodie whose double life inspired R.L. Stevenson's book 'Dr Jekyll and Mr Hyde'. A respected town councillor by day, Brodie led a gang of burglars by night, and was eventually caught and hanged in 1788, on a new style of gibbet that he, it is said, had designed.

The Royal Mile – High Street

The busy High Street is packed with places to explore, including many interesting closes and wynds, fascinating underground streets and vaults, and Parliament Square, Edinburgh's administrative, legal and ecclesiastical centre since the earliest times.

HEART OF MIDLOTHIAN

A heart-shaped design set in the cobbles marks the site of the entrance to the tolbooth that stood here for 400 years until it was demolished in 1817. The tolbooth served as a collection point for tolls and taxes, council chamber and courthouse, prison and place of execution.

JOHN KNOX c.1513–72

Originally a Roman Catholic priest, John Knox joined the Protestant reformers at St Andrew's Castle in c.1547 but, when it was captured by the French, was taken prisoner and served a year and a half as a galley slave. In 1549 he went to England and actively promoted the government's Protestant changes, but in 1553 the Roman Catholic Mary Tudor became queen and Knox fled to Geneva. Here he eagerly absorbed the harsh and humourless doctrines of Calvin, and wrote his famous attack on women in power, 'The First Blast of the Trumpet Against the Monstrous Regiment of Women'. Returning to Scotland in 1559 and appointed Minister of St Giles', Knox became the leader of the Protestant reformation, establishing a Calvinist Church. An aggressive spokesman of the new religion, he struck violently at the root of popery and was a bitter opponent of Mary Queen of Scots (▷19).

ST GILES' CATHEDRAL

Dominating the Old Town's skyline is St Giles' Cathedral's distinctive open-crown spire of 1495. Supporting the spire are four pillars dating from around 1120. These are part of an early church that was the responsibility of the Lazarites, who cared for lepers, and this may be why the church is dedicated to St Giles, patron saint of lepers. Edinburgh's High Kirk has suffered much change within, being divided into sections at times, and used as parliament house, court, police office and even prison. The exquisite and intricately carved Thistle Chapel was added in c.1910 as the religious home to The Order of the Thistle, Scotland's highest order of chivalry.

PARLIAMENT HOUSE

This was home to the Scottish Parliament until its dissolution in 1707, and is now the seat of the Scottish supreme courts. At certain times visitors may enter at No. 11 and view Parliament Hall, with its large stained-glass window and the magnificent hammer-beam roof under which the advocates and solicitors pace, discussing their cases.

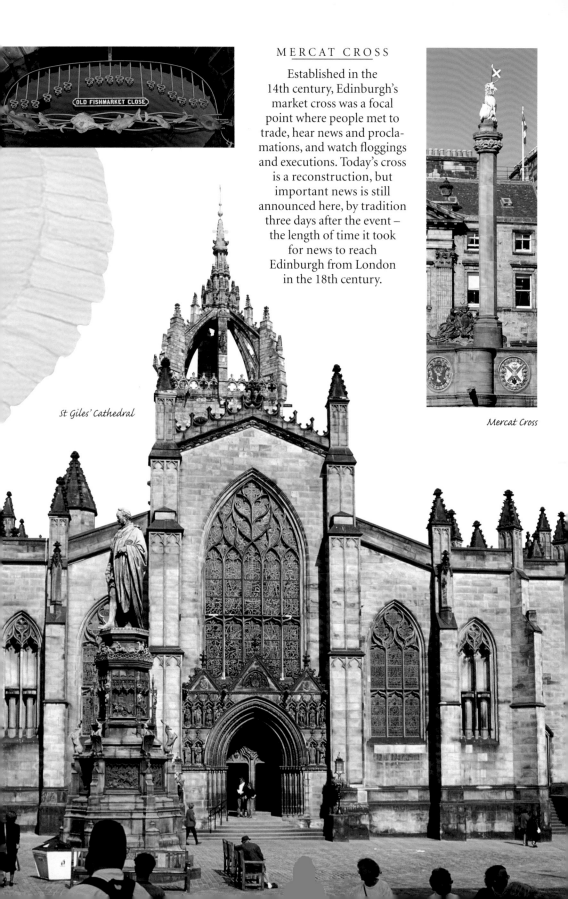

OLD FISHMARKET CLOSE

MERCAT CROSS

Established in the 14th century, Edinburgh's market cross was a focal point where people met to trade, hear news and proclamations, and watch floggings and executions. Today's cross is a reconstruction, but important news is still announced here, by tradition three days after the event – the length of time it took for news to reach Edinburgh from London in the 18th century.

St Giles' Cathedral

Mercat Cross

CITY CHAMBERS

This building was designed by John Adam and built in 1753–61 as the Royal Exchange. However, it failed to interest the merchants who preferred to do their business in the taverns, and was converted to chambers in 1811. Beneath the building is the 16th-century Mary King Close, the inhabitants of which died of the plague in 1645. The close can be visited on a special tour.

TRON KIRK

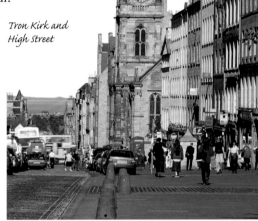

Tron Kirk and High Street

Named after the tron, a public weigh beam that stood nearby, this church was built in the 17th century over the 14th-century Marlin's Wynd, evidence of which can be seen inside. The church's original wooden tower was destroyed by fire in 1824, but its fine lattice-trussed roof remains.

PAISLEY CLOSE

An inscription above the entrance to this close refers to an incident in 1861 when a tenement collapsed at this point, killing 35 people. As rescuers were clearing through the rubble they heard a young survivor's voice cry out "Heave awa' chaps, I'm no' dead yet".

LITTLE TREATS IN EDINBURGH

- A 'trip down memory lane' at the Museum of Childhood (▷ 12).
- A bag of delicious fresh cream fudge from the Fudge House of Edinburgh in Canongate (▷ 14–15).
- The panoramic view from the Argyle Battery at the castle (▷ 4–5).
- A browse through local history at Huntly House Museum (▷ 15).
- A fascinating visit to the Camera Obscura (▷ 7).
- A tea or coffee break in the Laigh Coffee House in Hanover Street.
- Italian speciality food from Valvona and Crolla in Leith Walk, or a superb Italian breakfast in their café.
- A walk from Stockbridge to Dean Village beside the Water of Leith (▷ 28).

MUSEUM OF CHILDHOOD

Founded in 1955 by a town councillor who claimed to dislike children, this fascinating museum is crammed with playthings of bygone years and will delight children and adults alike.

MOUBRAY HOUSE

Thought to be one of the oldest dwellings in Edinburgh, Moubray House was once the home of Daniel Defoe, author of 'Robinson Crusoe'. In front stands one of the wells that supplied the Old Town with piped water. Residents collected their water in buckets, or had it delivered by a 'caddie' who carried it in a small barrel on his back.

JOHN KNOX HOUSE

Jutting into the road is John Knox House, saved from destruction by the popular myth that it was for a while the home of Scotland's famous religious reformer (▷ 10). This striking late 15th-century house was at one time owned by the wealthy James Mosman, goldsmith to Mary Queen of Scots. It contains an exhibition that tells John Knox's dramatic story.

BRASS RUBBING CENTRE

An intriguing collection of replicas of Pictish stones and medieval brasses are available for rubbing in Trinity Apse, situated in Chalmers' Close.

The Royal Mile – Canongate

The 12th-century Scottish King David I permitted the canons of Holyrood Abbey (▷ 18) to build houses on either side of the path, or 'gait', that led from their abbey to the Royal Burgh, and so the burgh of Canongate began, remaining separate from Edinburgh until 1856. Members of the royal court built large and grand houses in this fashionable area, but by the 1800s the elegant New Town (▷ 26–27) had proved too strong an attraction, and Canongate became deserted, deteriorating into an industrial slum which was not renovated until the 1950s.

MORAY HOUSE

Completed in 1625, this elegant mansion with twin pinnacles at its entrance was visited by Oliver Cromwell. In 1707 the beautiful gardens of Moray House were chosen for the signing of the Treaty of the Union, but fierce opposition caused the signatories to flee to a safer place.

Canongate Tolbooth

CANONGATE TOLBOOTH

Canongate's splendid civic centre, built in 1591, served as tax collection and municipal affairs centre, court and gaol. It now houses 'The People's Story', a museum of the lives, work and leisure of ordinary Edinburgh people from the late 18th century to the present day, featuring displays of memorabil from in and around the city.

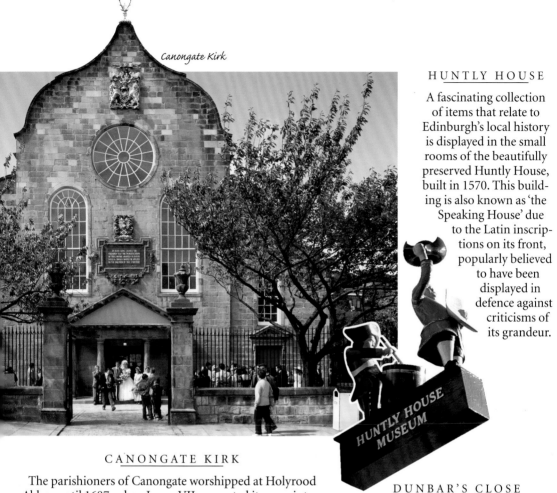

Canongate Kirk

HUNTLY HOUSE

A fascinating collection of items that relate to Edinburgh's local history is displayed in the small rooms of the beautifully preserved Huntly House, built in 1570. This building is also known as 'the Speaking House' due to the Latin inscriptions on its front, popularly believed to have been displayed in defence against criticisms of its grandeur.

CANONGATE KIRK

The parishioners of Canongate worshipped at Holyrood Abbey until 1687, when James VII converted its nave into a chapel for the Order of the Thistle. Canongate Kirk was built for them in 1688, and it is here that the Royal Family worships when residing at Holyrood.

DUNBAR'S CLOSE

A beautiful and secret 17th-century garden lies behind the busy Royal Mile in Dunbar's Close.

QUEENSBERRY HOUSE

The impressive Queensberry House, built in 1681, was once the home of the young and completely mad Lord Drumlanrig, who spit-roasted and ate the kitchen boy.

WHITE HORSE CLOSE

Extensively rebuilt in the last 80 years, this picturesque close was built as the White Horse Inn and coaching stables in 1623, on the site of the Royal Mews. In the 18th century the stagecoach to London left from here, arriving at its destination a week and a half later.

White Horse Close

Military Tattoo on the Castle Esplanade

16

Edinburgh Festival

For five weeks each summer Scotland's capital is taken over by the world's largest arts festival. Its vibrant and colourful atmosphere pervades the city, while every theatre and hall is filled with performances and every available wall covered with posters. On the streets bizarre and impromptu acts abound, providing free entertainment for the multi-national crowds that gather. Edinburgh's festival embodies the International Festival, the Fringe, the Military Tattoo and festivals of film, books and jazz. The International Festival, established over 50 years ago, draws together the world's finest performers of music, dance and drama, and on the Fringe hundreds of amateur and less-known professional groups compete for their audiences with irrepressible spirit and adventurous ideas. At the spectacular Military Tattoo, pipe bands and stunt groups perform on the Esplanade under floodlights against the dramatic backdrop of the castle.

WHAT'S ON

Full information on these annual events is available at the Edinburgh and Scotland Information Centre.

April	International Science Festival
May	International Children's Festival
June	Royal Highland Show
August	International Festival
	Festival Cavalcade
	Festival Fringe
	Military Tattoo
	International Book Festival
	International Film Festival
	International Jazz and Blues Festival
	West End Craft and Design Fair at St John's, Princes Street
September	Bank of Scotland Fireworks Concert in Princes Street Gardens
November	Shoots and Roots Folk Festival
December	Edinburgh's Hogmanay, 'the world's biggest New Year Party'

Fringe Sunday in Holyrood Park

Holyrood Palace

The Palace of Holyrood stands majestically at the end of the Royal Mile. Since the foundation of the abbey in 1128 by King David I, Holyrood has seen extensive development, vicious attack, glittering pageantry and violent murder. Today the official Scottish home of the Royal Family opens its door to visitors who wish to explore the elegant apartments and the gruesome history behind the palace's splendid façade.

ABBEY RUINS

A romantic story relating to David I's foundation of Holyrood Abbey tells of a hunting expedition in which the king fell from his horse and was attacked by a stag. As he wrestled with the beast a cross (or rood) appeared between its antlers, and when David grasped it the stag retreated. In gratitude for his divine deliverance he founded the monastery of the Holy Rood for a community of Augustinian monks. The ruined structure that remains today dates mainly from the 13th century.

Holyrood Abbey ruins

Holyrood Palace

THE PALACE

The marvellous palace of Holyrood originated as a guesthouse for royal visitors to the abbey. James IV started the transformation in 1501 when he prepared the residence for his new bride, Margaret Tudor, but the palace reached its present form in the 1670s when it was almost entirely rebuilt at the order of Charles II.

State apartments: King's Closet

MARY QUEEN OF SCOTS 1542–87

Queen before she was a week old, Mary was sent to Paris at the age of five and married the boy dauphin, Francis, when she was 15. Two years later Francis died, and Mary returned to Scotland a widow. She was popular with the Scots, and managed the difficult role of Catholic queen in a Protestant country with sensitivity. But in 1565 she married the young and selfish Lord Darnley, and just eight months later at Holyrood, Darnley, jealous of Mary's secretary and confidant David Rizzio, burst into her chamber with his conspirators, dragged Rizzio from the room and savagely stabbed him to death. Soon after the birth of Mary's son James VI, in 1566, Darnley was murdered. Barely three months later Mary married the Earl of Bothwell, the prime suspect in Darnley's death. Scotland was outraged, and Mary was soon imprisoned in Lochleven Castle and forced to abdicate in favour of her infant son. Escaping in 1568 she tried to regain the throne but, defeated, fled to England and spent 19 years in prison before being executed at the command of the Protestant English queen, Elizabeth.

VISITING THE PALACE

The historic apartments and the abbey ruins are open to the public unless the Royal Family in residence. Visitors are given an entertaining and informative guided tour which lasts approximately 45 minutes.

HOLYROOD PARK

This beautiful and extensive royal park offers many pleasant walks. The highest point in the park is Arthur's Seat, the central core of an extinct volcano. It is a stiff climb to the summit, but worthwhile for the magnificent panoramic views.

The Old Town

Steeped in intriguing and often gruesome history, Edinburgh's Old Town, with the Royal Mile (▷ 6–15) as its spine, grew up tightly crammed inside its defensive boundaries – the city wall skirting around the south and the Nor' Loch to the north. Though much of the Old Town degenerated into a crime-ridden slum when its more affluent residents were lured by the New Town (▷ 26–27), restoration has revived the area's picturesque and evocative charm.

ROBERT BURNS
1759–96

The son of an Ayrshire farmer, Burns found inspiration for his poetic gifts in the folk songs of the area. He worked as a farmer while writing poetry, and at the age of 27 visited Edinburgh, where he became something of a celebrity and was dubbed 'Caledonia's Bard'. He returned to farming two years later but when this failed he decided to enter the Excise Office. Burns died of rheumatic fever at the age of 37, and was buried with military honours.

VICTORIA STREET

Lined with unusual shops and cafés, this charming street is surmounted by Victoria Terrace, which leads through to the Lawnmarket (▷ 8–9).

Children selling shellfish, 1820

Victoria Street

Grassmarket

WEST BOW

In the 17th century West Bow was home to Major Thomas Weir, a pious Protestant who was often seen on the streets, leaning on a staff while delivering prayers and sermons. He shocked everyone when, one day, he broke down and confessed to a life of incest, bestiality and sorcery. He was burned along with the infamous staff, which proved reluctant to ignite.

GRASSMARKET

The broad and leafy Grassmarket was the site of a regular market for over 400 years, and the scene of many a public execution. From 1661 until 1688 many Covenanters were hanged here, and in 1736 John Porteous, captain of the city guard, was lynched in the famous Porteous Riots after he had ordered his men to fire on a disorderly crowd.

It was from the Grassmarket that the notorious Burke and Hare operated: they murdered 16 people by strangulation and sold their bodies to the University Medical School for dissection.

The Old Town

GREYFRIARS' BOBBY

A bronze statue at the top of Candlemaker Row commemorates Bobby, a Skye terrier who belonged to John Gray, the local policeman. When Bobby was just two, Gray died and was buried in Greyfriars Kirkyard. Bobby refused to go far from his master's grave, venturing to the local tavern each lunchtime, to be fed. He continued to keep his vigil for 14 years, until he died in 1872. Bobby was buried in the churchyard not far from his master. His collar and bowl are displayed in Huntly House Museum (▷ 15).

Greyfriars' Bobby

GREYFRIARS KIRK

Opened in 1620, this church was the first to be built in Scotland after the Reformation. It suffered damage when it was taken over by Cromwell's troops as barracks in the 1650s, and later in 1718 when its tower exploded due to gunpowder stored there by the city fathers. It was in Greyfriars Kirkyard, in 1638, that the first signatures were put to the National Covenant, a document declaring opposition to the 'papist' religion. The churchyard contains many grand monuments to distinguished people, but the graves that excite the most interest are those of John Gray and his dog Bobby.

Holyrood Road

DYNAMIC EARTH

This vibrant, interactive exhibition takes visitors on an exciting journey of discovery back through time and explains, in virtual reality, the formation of the planet Earth.

Dynamic Earth

SCOTTISH PARLIAMENT

The new Scottish Parliament building, under construction at the east end of Holyrood Road, opens in 2003. In the meantime, information on the Scottish Parliament is available at the Visitor Centre, situated in the Committee Chambers Building on George IV Bridge.

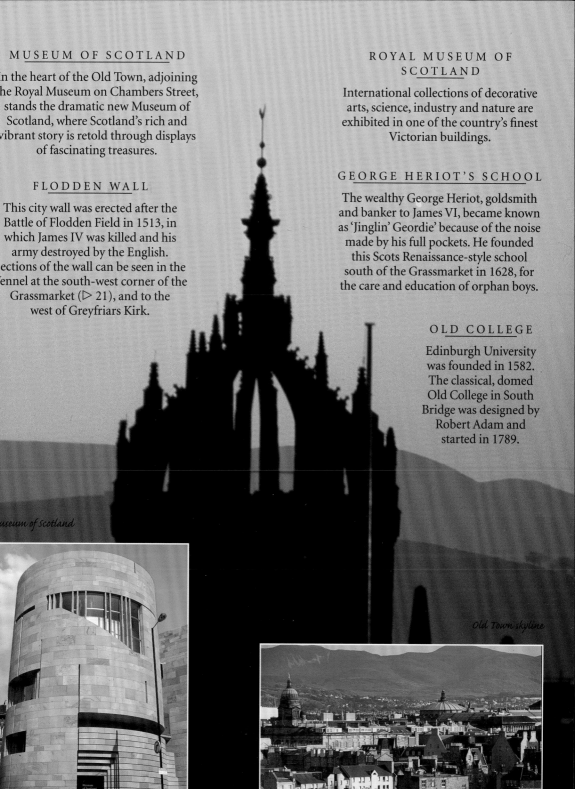

MUSEUM OF SCOTLAND

In the heart of the Old Town, adjoining the Royal Museum on Chambers Street, stands the dramatic new Museum of Scotland, where Scotland's rich and vibrant story is retold through displays of fascinating treasures.

FLODDEN WALL

This city wall was erected after the Battle of Flodden Field in 1513, in which James IV was killed and his army destroyed by the English. Sections of the wall can be seen in the Vennel at the south-west corner of the Grassmarket (▷ 21), and to the west of Greyfriars Kirk.

ROYAL MUSEUM OF SCOTLAND

International collections of decorative arts, science, industry and nature are exhibited in one of the country's finest Victorian buildings.

GEORGE HERIOT'S SCHOOL

The wealthy George Heriot, goldsmith and banker to James VI, became known as 'Jinglin' Geordie' because of the noise made by his full pockets. He founded this Scots Renaissance-style school south of the Grassmarket in 1628, for the care and education of orphan boys.

OLD COLLEGE

Edinburgh University was founded in 1582. The classical, domed Old College in South Bridge was designed by Robert Adam and started in 1789.

Museum of Scotland

Old Town skyline

Princes Street

Edinburgh's main shopping street, this remarkable boulevard was built as part of the New Town, and is distinctive in that it has shops on only the north side, allowing unobstructed views of the Old Town's skyline and the castle.

REGISTER HOUSE

Started by Robert Adam in 1774, Register House, at the east end of Princes Street, has a magnificent domed ceiling which visitors are welcome to view. In front of the building stands the impressive bronze equestrian statue of the Duke of Wellington, victor of the Battle of Waterloo.

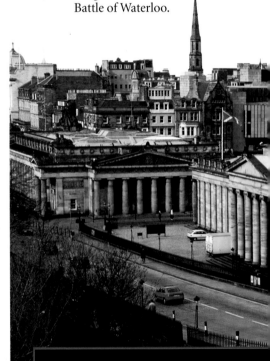

SCOTT MONUMENT

Scotland's most patriotic and influential writer is commemorated in this towering Victorian Gothic pile, intricately carved with statuettes of characters from Scott's novels. Visitors prepared to climb the 287 spiral steps to the top are rewarded with stunning views.

SIR WALTER SCOTT 1771–1832

Edinburgh-born Scott lived in George Square until he was 26, suffering as a young child from poliomyelitis, which left him lame for the rest of his life. Never an outstanding scholar, his particular interest was in historic literature. He lived with his wife in various houses in the New Town until 1804, and from that time became a prolific writer of poems and romantic novels, including 'Ivanhoe'. His writing was deeply patriotic and captured the imagination of Queen Victoria, who started the annual royal visits to Balmoral and Holyrood.

ROYAL SCOTTISH ACADEMY

This superb neo-classical building is designed by William Playfair, one of Edinburgh's most influential 19th-century architects. The gallery houses major exhibitions.

NATIONAL GALLERY

Also by Playfair, the 1854 National Gallery houses the national collections of European and Scottish art from the Renaissance to the Post-Impressionist period, including masterpieces by Gauguin, Van Gogh, Ramsay and Raeburn.

THE MOUND

Soil and rubble from the New Town's foundations were used to create a convenient link between Princes Street and the high ridge of the Royal Mile.

al Scottish Academy and National Gallery

A painting of Edinburgh Castle and Nor' Loch by Alexander Nasmyth

PRINCES STREET GARDENS

In 1460 the Nor' Loch was created in this area. Intended for the defence of the Old Town, it was also used for the disposal of house-hold waste and the ducking of law-breakers. In 1759 the loch was drained in preparation for the building of the New Town, and the city was left with a stinking marsh until the area was filled in with earth from the foundations of Princes Street buildings. A private garden created here in 1818 was opened to the public 60 years later.

Now the attractive gardens provide a relaxing escape from the noisy street, and are worth exploring for the statues, the special gardens and the floral clock with a mechanical cuckoo.

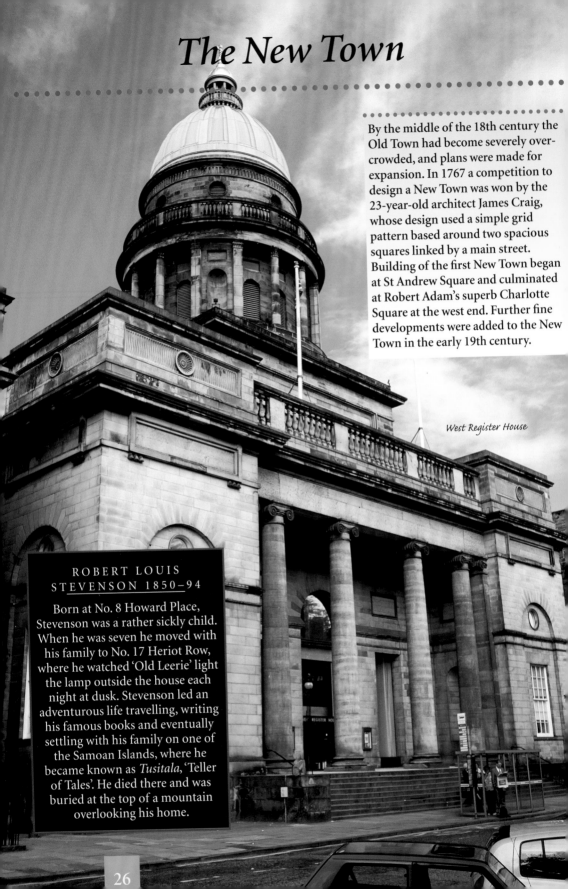

The New Town

By the middle of the 18th century the Old Town had become severely over-crowded, and plans were made for expansion. In 1767 a competition to design a New Town was won by the 23-year-old architect James Craig, whose design used a simple grid pattern based around two spacious squares linked by a main street. Building of the first New Town began at St Andrew Square and culminated at Robert Adam's superb Charlotte Square at the west end. Further fine developments were added to the New Town in the early 19th century.

West Register House

ROBERT LOUIS STEVENSON 1850–94

Born at No. 8 Howard Place, Stevenson was a rather sickly child. When he was seven he moved with his family to No. 17 Heriot Row, where he watched 'Old Leerie' light the lamp outside the house each night at dusk. Stevenson led an adventurous life travelling, writing his famous books and eventually settling with his family on one of the Samoan Islands, where he became known as *Tusitala*, 'Teller of Tales'. He died there and was buried at the top of a mountain overlooking his home.

Royal Bank of Scotland

NATIONAL PORTRAIT GALLERY

Situated at the east end of Queen Street and housed in an imposing neo-Gothic building of the 1880s, the Portrait Gallery displays images of Scots who have influenced their country's history.

GEORGE STREET

Running along the crest of a ridge and forming the spine of the New Town, George Street is noted for its superb Classical and Renaissance façades. The church of St Andrew and St George is oval in shape ('so the devil cannae hide in corners') and features a fine ceiling. The gracious Assembly Rooms were built in 1787 as a venue for formal dances. An unexpected view of the Firth of Forth can be enjoyed at the junction with Hanover Street.

ST ANDREW SQUARE

Originally a residential area, this square is now said to be the richest square in Europe due to the number of bank and insurance company offices it contains. A magnificent town house built in 1772 is now used by the Royal Bank of Scotland, and its stunning, star-spangled cupola roof can be viewed by the public.

Moray Estate

MORAY ESTATE

Built on the Earl of Moray's estate in the 1820s to the highest specifications, the Moray Estate was designed by James Gillespie Graham using attractive curved crescents and circuses joined by short avenues.

The Georgian House

CHARLOTTE SQUARE

esigned by Robert Adam in 1791 with imposing palatial açades on two sides and the superb West Register House originally a church), Charlotte Square (above) is consid-ed a masterpiece. The Georgian House at No. 7 has been furnished and decorated in the style of its time by The National Trust for Scotland. The statue of Albert at the centre of the square pleased Queen Victoria so greatly that she knighted its sculptor immediately.

Out of the Centre

Visitors who have time to venture beyond the city centre will find some of Edinburgh's finest attractions, including the fascinating and unique residential areas that were once outlying villages.

Edinburgh Zoo

DEAN VILLAGE

Nestled in a wooded valley below Queensferry Street is the peaceful little village of Dean. From the 12th century this was a milling community, running eleven watermills and two granaries. Vestiges of this age remain, including, at the bottom of Bell's Brae, a bakers' symbol on the old bakers' meeting house, and the Baxters' Tolbooth. Spanning the valley is Thomas Telford's mighty bridge, completed in 1832.

Dean Village

BRITANNIA

The famous and splendid former royal yacht, *Britann* which carried the Royal Family on 968 official voya over a period of 44 years, now berthed at Leith. Edir burgh's ancient port, Leit remained a separate burg until 1920, and still retains individual character, with many of its old waterfron buildings being refurbishe as restaurants and bars.

WATER OF LEITH WALKWAY

The delightful riverside path that leaves north-east from Dean Village takes walkers past St Bernard's Well, a small Greek temple to Hygeia that was once a mineral spring, and on to Stockbridge, a charming residential area developed in the early 19th century.

Britannia

Leith

EDINBURGH ZOO

Set in hillside parkland just over two miles from the city centre, ~~E~~dinburgh's spacious and delightful ~~z~~oo offers a great day out for all the ~~fa~~mily. Edinburgh's penguins boast the biggest penguin enclosure in ~~th~~e world, and in summer take part in a daily penguin parade.

NATIONAL GALLERY OF MODERN ART

~~W~~orks by major modern artists are ~~sh~~own in the gallery's bright spacious ~~ro~~oms, while the grounds provide an ideal setting for sculptures. The ~~g~~allery is situated in Belford Road.

Royal Botanic Garden

FORTH BRIDGE

When the Forth Railway Bridge was opened in 1890 it was the biggest bridge in the world, and considered the engineering wonder of its age. ~~Pa~~inters work continuously to preserve the bridge's ~~m~~etalwork, starting again at the beginning as soon as they have reached the end. Visitors may also admire the road bridge, see the Queensferry Museum, or sail on the *Maid of the Forth* to ~~In~~chcolm Island which has a bird sanctuary, ruins ~~of~~ an Augustinian abbey and visiting grey seals.

ROYAL BOTANIC GARDEN

Situated just a short bus ride from the bustling city centre is Edinburgh's superb botanic garden, known to be one of the finest in the world. It was founded in 1670 when two Edinburgh physicians began to grow medicinal plants on a small plot of land near Holyrood Palace, and was eventually moved to its present site at Inverleith in the 1820s. Restful and rejuvenating, the garden includes a colourful rhododendron walk, a fine rock garden and superb glasshouses.

Calton Hill

Rising up at the east end of Princes Street is Calton Hill which, dotted with Greek-style monuments and follies, contributes to Edinburgh's title, 'the Athens of the North'. The climb to the top is not too arduous, and the panoramic views in all directions are exhilarating.

NELSON MONUMENT

Designed by Robert Burn to look like an upturned telescope, this monument features on its top a time-ball which drops to the bottom of its staff at one o'clock each day. Visitors may climb the spiral stairs to the lookout tower.

OLD OBSERVATORY

Designed in the style of a Gothic fortress by James Craig, architect of the first New Town (▷ 26–27), and completed in 1792, this was the first building on Calton Hill.

Nelson Monument

DUGALD STEWART

A circular, Grecian temple-style monument by Playfair commemorates Dugald Stewart, late 18th-century Scottish philosopher.

NATIONAL MONUMENT

Playfair's monument to those who fell in the Napoleonic Wars, designed to be a replica of the Parthenon at Athens, was left unfinished in the 1820s when funds ran out.

CITY OBSERVATORY

William Playfair designed this cross-shaped, Roman Doric-style observatory in 1818.

Calton

BURNS MONUMENT

A handsome monument to Scotland's famous bard, Robert Burns (▷ 20), stands in Regent Road on the southern slope of Calton Hill.

National Gallery

MUSEUMS AND GALLERIES

City Art Centre:
0131 529 3993
Dean Gallery:
0131 624 6200
Dynamic Earth:
(▷ 22)   0131 550 7800
Fruitmarket Gallery:
0131 225 2383
Georgian House:
(▷ 27)   0131 226 3318
Gladstone's Land:
(▷ 9)   0131 226 5856
John Knox House:
(▷ 13)   0131 556 9579
Huntly House Museum:
(▷ 15)   0131 529 4143
Museum of Childhood:
(▷ 12)   0131 529 4142
Museum of Scotland:
(▷ 23)   0131 247 4422
National Gallery of Scotland:
(▷ 25)   0131 624 6200
The People's Story:
(▷ 14)   0131 529 4057
Royal Museum of Scotland:
(▷ 23)   0131 225 7534
Scottish National Gallery of Modern Art:
(▷ 29)   0131 624 6200
Scottish National Portrait Gallery:
(▷ 27)   0131 624 6200
Writers' Museum:
(▷ 9)   0131 529 4901

WALKS AND TOURS

Edinburgh is best explored on foot, and many **guided walks** are available, from literary tours to spine-chilling ghost tours through the haunted Old Town and its underground vaults.
Open-top buses giving a guided tour of Edinburgh can be boarded at Waverley Bridge, or at any of their route stops.
Coach tours run from Edinburgh to many famous Scottish locations such as Loch Ness, Glencoe and Stirling Castle.
Details of all walks and tours can be found at the Edinburgh and Scotland Information Centre.

City Centre Plan

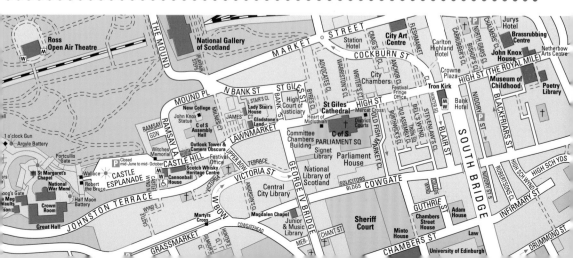

City Plan

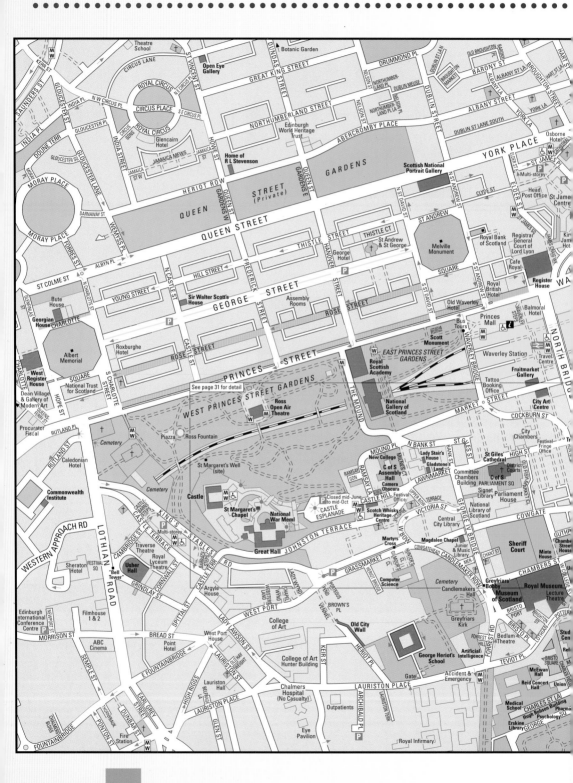